# YOUR COMPLETE ARIES 2024 PERSONAL HOROSCOPE

Monthly Astrological Prediction Forecast Readings of Every Zodiac Astrology Sun Star Signs- Love, Romance, Money, Finances, Career, Health, Travel, Spirituality.

Iris Quinn

Alpha Zuriel Publishing

Copyright © 2023 by **Iris Quinn**

All rights reserved. No part of this publication may be reproduced, distributed or transmitted in any form or by any means, without prior written permission.

**Alpha Zuriel Publishing
United States.**

The content contained within this book may not be reproduced, duplicated or transmitted without direct written permission from the author or the publisher.
Under no circumstances will any blame or legal responsibility be held against the publisher, or author, for any damages, reparation, or monetary loss due to the information contained within this book; either directly or indirectly.

Legal Notice:
This book is copyright protected. This book is only for personal use. You cannot amend, distribute, sell, use, quote or paraphrase any part, or the content within this book, without the consent of the author or publisher.

Disclaimer Notice:
Please note the information contained within this document is for educational and entertainment purposes only. All effort has been executed to present accurate, up to date, and reliable, complete information. No warranties of any kind are declared or implied. Readers acknowledge that the author is not engaging in the rendering of legal, financial, medical or professional advice.

**Your Complete Aries 2024 Personal Horoscope/ Iris Quinn**. -- 1st ed.

*"In the dance of the planets, we find the rhythms of life. Astrology reminds us that we are all connected to the greater universe, and our actions have ripple effects throughout the cosmos."*
— IRIS QUINN

# CONTENTS

ARIES PROFILE ............................................................. 1
   PERSONALITY OF ARIES ................................. 5
   WEAKNESSES OF ARIES ................................. 7
   RELATIONSHIP COMPATIBILITY WITH ARIES ..................................................................... 10
   LOVE AND PASSION ........................................ 17
   MARRIAGE ......................................................... 21
ARIES 2024 HOROSCOPE ............................................ 23
   Overview Aries 2024 ............................................ 23
   January 2024 ........................................................ 27
   February 2024 ...................................................... 37
   March 2024 ........................................................... 48
   April 2024 ............................................................. 57
   May 2024 .............................................................. 63
   June 2024 .............................................................. 69
   July 2024 ............................................................... 74
   August 2024 ......................................................... 79
   September 2024 .................................................... 84
   October 2024 ........................................................ 89
   November 2024 .................................................... 97
   December 2024 .................................................. 108

CHAPTER ONE

# ARIES PROFILE

- Constellation: Aries
- Zodiac symbol: Ram
- Date: March 20 – April 19
- Element: Fire
- Ruling Planet: Mars
- Career Planet: Saturn
- Love Planet: Venus
- Money Planet: Venus
- Planet of Fun, Entertainment, Creativity, and Speculations: Sun
- Planet of Health and Work: Mercury
- Planet of Home and Family Life: Moon
- Planet of Spirituality: Neptune
- Planet of Travel, Education, Religion, and Philosophy: Jupiter

Colors:
- Colors: Carmine, Red, Scarlet
- Colors that promote love, romance, and social harmony: Green, Jade Green
- Color that promotes earning power: Green

Gem: Amethyst Metals: Iron, Steel
Scent: Honeysuckle
Birthstone: Diamond

Qualities:
- Quality: Cardinal (represents activity)
- Quality most needed for balance: Caution.

Strongest Virtues:
- Abundant physical energy
- Courage
- Honesty
- Independence
- Self-reliance

Deepest Need: Action

Characteristics to Avoid:
- Haste
- Impetuousness
- Over-aggression

- Rashness

Signs of Greatest Overall Compatibility:
- Leo
- Sagittarius

Signs of Greatest Overall Incompatibility:
- Cancer
- Libra
- Capricorn

  - Sign Most Supportive for Career Advancement: Capricorn
  - Sign Most Supportive for Emotional Well-being: Cancer
  - Sign Most Supportive Financially: Taurus
  - Sign Best for Marriage and/or Partnerships: Libra
  - Sign Most Supportive for Creative Projects: Leo
  - Best Sign to Have Fun With: Leo
  - Signs Most Supportive in Spiritual Matters: Sagittarius, Pisces

Best Day of the Week: Tuesday

## ARIES TRAITS

- Bold and courageous
- Energetic and action-oriented
- Independent and self-reliant
- Passionate and driven.
- Adventurous and willing to take risks.
- Direct and straightforward in communication
- Quick to start new projects and initiatives.
- Competitive and determined to succeed.
- Impulsive and spontaneous
- Enthusiastic and optimistic
- Dynamic and assertive
- Fierce and protective of their loved ones

## PERSONALITY OF ARIES

Aries individuals have a dynamic and energetic personality. They possess a natural zest for life and thrive on action and excitement. With their bold and courageous nature, they are not afraid to take risks and face challenges head-on. Aries is known for their independent and self-reliant character, valuing their freedom and autonomy. They have a strong sense of self and are often natural-born leaders.

Impulsiveness and spontaneity are common traits of Aries individuals. They tend to act on their instincts and follow their passions without overthinking. Aries has a competitive spirit and a strong desire to excel in everything they do. They approach life with enthusiasm and determination, never shying away from a challenge.

Directness is a hallmark of Aries communication style. They are straightforward and say what's on their mind without sugar-coating. Aries is passionate and fiery, bringing an intense energy to their endeavors and relationships. However, their quick temper can sometimes lead to moments of anger or frustration, which they may soon forget and move on from.

Aries individuals are fiercely loyal and protective of their loved ones. They are ready to defend and support those they care about, showing unwavering commitment. With their vibrant and enthusiastic personality, Aries has a natural ability to inspire and motivate others.

Overall, the personality of an Aries can be described as bold, energetic, independent, impulsive, passionate, and protective. These traits contribute to their dynamic and influential presence in both personal and professional aspects of life.

## WEAKNESSES OF ARIES

Aries individuals, like everyone else, have certain weaknesses to be aware of. It's important to note that these weaknesses are not necessarily inherent in every Aries, and individuals may vary in their experiences and characteristics. Some common weaknesses associated with Aries include:

Impatience: Aries individuals can be known for their impatience. They may have a strong desire to see immediate results and may become frustrated when things don't progress as quickly as they would like. This impatience can sometimes lead to impulsive decision-making or a lack of tolerance for delays.

Quick-Tempered: Aries can have a fiery temperament and a quick temper. They may be prone to becoming easily angered or frustrated, sometimes resulting in conflicts or heated arguments. It's important for Aries individuals to learn to manage their emotions and find constructive ways to express their frustrations.

Impulsiveness: Aries individuals tend to act on their impulses and instincts. While this can bring excitement and spontaneity into their lives, it can also lead to impulsive decisions or actions that they may later regret. It's important for Aries to take a moment to pause and consider the potential consequences before acting impulsively.

Self-Centeredness: Due to their independent and self-reliant nature, Aries individuals may sometimes prioritize their own desires and needs above others. They may need to be mindful of considering the perspectives and feelings of those around them and practice empathy and understanding in their interactions.

Restlessness: Aries individuals have a high energy level and a need for constant stimulation and activity. They can become easily bored with routine tasks and may seek new challenges and adventures. However, this restlessness can sometimes make it difficult for them to stay focused or see long-term projects through to completion.

Over-Competitiveness: Aries individuals have a strong competitive drive and a desire to be the best. While this can fuel their motivation and drive for success, it can also lead to excessive focus on winning or outperforming others. Aries individuals may need to strike a balance between healthy competition and cooperation in their personal and professional relationships.

It's important to remember that these weaknesses are not universal for all Aries individuals, and individual experiences may vary. Awareness of these potential challenges can help Aries individuals navigate them more effectively and cultivate personal growth.

# RELATIONSHIP COMPATIBILITY WITH ARIES

Based only on their Sun signs, this is how Aries interacts with others. These are the compatibility interpretations for all 12 potential Aries combinations. This is a limited and insufficient method of determining compatibility. However, Sun-sign compatibility remains the foundation for overall harmony in a relationship.

The general rule is that yin and yang do not get along. Yin complements yin, and yang complements yang. While yin and yang partnerships can be successful, they require more effort. Earth and water zodiac signs are both Yin. Yang is represented by the fire and air zodiac signs.

*Aries (Yang) and Aries (Yang)*

When two Aries come together, it can be a dynamic and passionate union. Both share similar traits, including their assertiveness, enthusiasm, and adventurous spirit. Their relationship can be filled with excitement, spontaneity, and a shared drive for new experiences. However, conflicts may arise due to their strong-willed nature and desire for independence. Both individuals will need to find a balance between asserting their individuality and compromising for the sake of the relationship. With open communication and mutual respect, they can create a fiery and exhilarating partnership, fueling each other's passions and supporting each other's goals.

*Aries (Yang) and Taurus (Yin)*

Aries' fiery energy can ignite Taurus' grounded and sensual nature. They can create a harmonious balance between Aries' passion and Taurus' stability, nurturing a relationship with excitement and stability. Aries' drive can inspire Taurus' determination, while Taurus can provide a calming influence on Aries' intensity.

*Aries (Yang) and Gemini (Yin)*

Aries' drive and enthusiasm complement Gemini's adaptable and communicative nature. Together, they can enjoy a dynamic and intellectually stimulating partnership, keeping the relationship vibrant and evolving. Aries' passion can energize Gemini's curiosity, while Gemini can provide intellectual stimulation and social versatility.

### *Aries (Yang) and Cancer (Yin)*

Aries and Cancer have different emotional needs and communication styles, which can lead to misunderstandings and conflicts. Aries' directness may clash with Cancer's sensitivity, and Cancer's desire for security and emotional connection may clash with Aries' need for independence. They will need to work on understanding and respecting each other's emotional needs to find harmony in the relationship.

### *Aries (Yang) and Leo (Yin)*

Aries and Leo share a fiery connection, both seeking adventure and recognition. Their combined energies create a passionate and vibrant relationship, with Aries' assertiveness complemented by Leo's warmth and generosity. Aries can fuel Leo's self-confidence and inspire them to pursue their passions, while Leo can provide admiration and encouragement for Aries' endeavors.

## COMPLETE ARIES 2024 PERSONAL HOROSCOPE

*Aries (Yang) and Virgo (Yin)*

Aries' boldness and Virgo's practicality may seem different at first, but they can find compatibility through mutual respect. Aries' energy can inspire Virgo's attention to detail, creating a harmonious partnership that balances action and thoughtfulness. Aries can encourage Virgo to step out of their comfort zone, while Virgo can offer practicality and groundedness to support Aries' ambitions.

*Aries (Yang) and Libra (Yin)*

Aries and Libra can have a challenging dynamic due to their different needs and approaches to relationships. Aries is more independent and assertive, while Libra seeks harmony and balance. Aries' directness and impulsive nature may clash with Libra's desire for peace and compromise. Both signs will need to find ways to navigate their differences and communicate effectively to maintain a balanced and harmonious relationship.

*Aries (Yang) and Scorpio (Yin)*

Aries' boldness meets Scorpio's depth and intensity. They can create a transformative and passionate relationship, with Aries' drive matched by Scorpio's emotional depth and loyalty. Aries can ignite Scorpio's passion and challenge them to explore their desires, while Scorpio can offer loyalty and intensity to fuel Aries' ambitions.

*Aries (Yang) and Sagittarius (Yin)*

Aries and Sagittarius share a mutual love for adventure and exploration. Their energies combine to create an exciting and dynamic partnership, where Aries' determination is balanced by Sagittarius' optimism and philosophical nature. Aries can provide the drive and motivation to pursue new experiences, while Sagittarius can bring wisdom and expansive thinking to support Aries' goals.

*Aries (Yang) and Capricorn (Yin)*

Aries and Capricorn have different approaches to life and may have conflicting priorities. Aries is spontaneous and action-oriented, while Capricorn is more cautious and focused on long-term goals. This difference in energy and outlook can lead to clashes and misunderstandings. Both signs will need to find common ground and appreciate each other's strengths to build a harmonious relationship.

*Aries (Yang) and Aquarius (Yin)*

Aries and Aquarius bring their individuality together, forming a unique and intellectually stimulating bond. Aries' passion and Aquarius' visionary thinking can create a relationship that embraces innovation and growth. Aries can provide the drive and motivation to turn Aquarius' ideas into reality, while Aquarius can offer intellectual stimulation and a sense of independence to fuel Aries' ambitions.

*Aries (Yang) and Pisces (Yin)*

Aries' assertiveness meets Pisces' sensitivity and intuition. They can form a relationship where Aries' drive is tempered by Pisces' compassion and emotional depth, creating a harmonious union of passion and empathy. Aries can bring strength and protection to Pisces' vulnerability, while Pisces can offer empathy and understanding to support Aries' emotional needs.

## LOVE AND PASSION

Aries individuals embody a passionate and energetic approach when it comes to love and relationships. Their vibrant personality infuses their romantic connections with a distinct sense of excitement and intensity. Here's a glimpse into the love and passion that drives the Aries personality, while also acknowledging some areas that may require attention:

Aries approaches love fearlessly, unafraid to take the lead and pursue the object of their affection with unwavering determination. Their assertiveness and confidence make them proactive in expressing their feelings and making their romantic intentions known. However, it is important for Aries to balance their assertiveness with sensitivity to ensure that their partner's needs and feelings are also considered.

When it comes to matters of the heart, Aries is known for their intense passion. They wholeheartedly invest themselves in their relationships, bringing a fiery energy that ignites deep emotional and physical connections. However, Aries should be mindful of the need for emotional balance and avoid overwhelming their partner with their intensity.

Spontaneity and adventure are essential elements in an Aries' love life. They thrive on surprises and enjoy creating memorable experiences for their partners. This zest for life keeps their relationships exciting and dynamic. However, Aries should also appreciate the importance of stability and consistency to ensure a solid foundation in their love life.

Loyalty is a cornerstone of Aries' love. Once committed, they fiercely protect and stand by their loved ones through thick and thin. Aries prioritizes the happiness and well-being of their partners, often going above and beyond to support and defend them. However, it's important for Aries to strike a balance between their loyalty and the need for individuality and personal space.

While being deeply devoted, Aries also values their independence within a relationship. They appreciate a partner who respects their need for personal space and autonomy. Aries seeks a balance between being a passionate, dedicated partner and maintaining their individuality and personal interests. However, they should be mindful of not becoming too focused on their own needs, and remember to nurture the needs of their partner as well.

Aries' love life is marked by the excitement and dynamism they bring to their relationships. They possess a natural magnetism that draws others to them. Their passionate nature, combined with their enthusiasm and zest for life, creates an electric atmosphere that keeps their love alive and vibrant.

However, Aries should also be aware of the importance of stability and consistency to sustain long-term relationships.

Honest and direct communication is highly valued by Aries in their relationships. They believe in open dialogue and expect their partners to reciprocate their level of candor. Aries appreciates a deep and meaningful connection where emotions can be freely expressed. However, they should also be mindful of their delivery and considerate of their partner's sensitivities.

An Aries seeks a partner who shares their sense of adventure and is willing to embark on thrilling experiences together. They desire a companion who can match their energy and enthusiasm, someone who can keep up with their dynamic and passionate nature. However, Aries should also value the importance of compromise and find ways to navigate differences with their partner.

Love for an Aries is an emotionally intense experience. They wear their hearts on their sleeves and invest themselves fully in their relationships. Aries seeks reciprocation, desiring a partner who can match their level of emotional involvement and create a profound connection. However, Aries should also be mindful of their partner's emotional needs and practice empathy and understanding.

## MARRIAGE

To keep an Aries individual happy in a marriage, it is essential to maintain a sense of spontaneity and avoid falling into a routine. Aries thrives on activity, variety, and stimulation, and they appreciate partners who can keep up with their energetic nature. While they are known for their adventurous spirit, Aries individuals are typically loyal and committed to their relationships.

When it comes to Aries men, they can sometimes struggle with strong and independent women due to their natural inclination towards being macho. However, many Aries men are confident enough to recognize the importance of a partner with character. They understand the value of giving their significant other the freedom and support they need to thrive.

On the other hand, Aries women are often perceived as challenging to deal with. They possess a dictatorial streak and may prefer a passive partner who allows them to take the lead and make decisions. However, these types of relationships rarely last because Aries women desire a powerful and confident mate who can match their level of strength without overpowering them.

But here's the secret: Those who manage to break through the initial barriers and truly connect with an Aries individual will discover a loyal and loving companion. Aries individuals are fiercely devoted to their partners and will go to great lengths to keep the relationship alive and thriving. Their zest for life and unwavering joy will uplift and inspire those who choose to embark on this fiery journey of love with them.

CHAPTER TWO

# ARIES 2024 HOROSCOPE

## Overview Aries 2024

Dear Aries, as you step into the year 2024, the cosmos is aligning in a way that will shape your journey in profound ways. The planetary movements throughout the year indicate a time of opportunities, challenges, and growth. The alignment of Mercury, Uranus, Sun, Venus, Mars, Jupiter, Saturn, Neptune, Chiron, and Pluto will play a crucial role in various aspects of your life, including your career, relationships, health, and personal development. Let's delve deeper into what the year has in store for you.

The year begins with Mercury in Taurus forming a semi-square with Neptune in Pisces in late May, suggesting a period of potential confusion or misunderstanding at work. It's important to communicate clearly and honestly during this time and to seek clarity when needed. The Sun in Gemini forming a semi-square with Chiron in Aries in late May also suggests that healing and recovery may be themes in your professional life at this time.

In June, Mercury in Taurus forms a sextile with Saturn in Pisces, indicating a period of stability and potential growth in your financial situation. This is a good time to invest or save money. However, the square between Venus and Uranus in August suggests potential unexpected expenses or financial changes. It's important to be prepared for these potential fluctuations and to manage your finances wisely.

In terms of relationships and social life, the square between Venus and Neptune in June indicates a time of confusion or misunderstanding in your relationships. It's important to communicate clearly and honestly during this time and to seek clarity when needed. The sextile between Mercury and the True Node in June also suggests that communication and social interactions will be particularly important during this time. This is a good time to build and strengthen relationships.

As the year progresses, you will find that your social life picks up pace. There is a sense of camaraderie and belonging that envelops you. Engage in social activities, but be mindful of not overcommitting yourself. Balance is key.

Your health and wellness are areas that require attention this year. The sesquiquadrate between the Sun and Chiron in June is a call for healing. This is the time to integrate wellness practices into your daily routine. Whether it's through yoga, meditation, or simply spending time in nature, nurturing your well-being is essential.

The latter part of the year brings vitality. The sextile between the Sun and Chiron in June is a rejuvenating energy. Engage in physical activities that not only strengthen your body but also bring joy to your soul.

On a spiritual level, 2024 is a year of profound growth and learning. The quintile between Jupiter and Saturn in May is a cosmic classroom. This is a time of spiritual learning and seeking higher wisdom. You are being called to delve deeper into the mysteries of life.

The conjunction between Venus and Pluto in July is a catalyst for transformation. This is a period of shedding old skins and emerging anew. Embrace the changes and allow yourself to grow and evolve.

# COMPLETE ARIES 2024 PERSONAL HOROSCOPE

In conclusion, Aries, the year 2024 will be a year of growth, transformation, and self-discovery. While there will be challenges along the way, these challenges will provide opportunities for personal development and understanding. Embrace the journey and make the most of the opportunities that come your way. Stay open to learning and growing, and don't be afraid to explore new paths. Your adventurous spirit will guide you through the ups and downs of the year, leading you to new heights in your personal and professional life.

Remember, the stars are merely guides. You have the power to shape your destiny. Use the insights from your horoscope to navigate the year, but always listen to your inner voice. It is your most reliable guide. Here's to a year filled with growth, success, and happiness.

# January 2024

Horoscope:

Dear Aries, welcome to the exciting month of January 2024! This month is filled with astrological aspects that will have a significant impact on various aspects of your life. You may experience a mix of challenges and opportunities, allowing you to grow and evolve.

The month kicks off with a Venus square Saturn aspect on January 1st. This alignment brings some tension and obstacles in your relationships and financial matters. However, it also encourages you to take a realistic approach and make necessary adjustments to find stability and long-term satisfaction.

On January 3rd, Venus forms a quincunx aspect with Jupiter, indicating a need for balance between your personal desires and your responsibilities. It's essential to find harmony between your ambitions and your relationships during this time.

Mercury's quintile with Saturn on the same day enhances your communication skills and intellectual capabilities. It's a favorable time for planning, organizing, and focusing on your long-term goals.

Throughout the month, Mars, the planet of action and energy, interacts with Pluto, Neptune, and Uranus, bringing a dynamic mix of transformative energy, inspiration, and unexpected changes. This combination fuels your motivation and intensifies your drive to achieve your aspirations.

The Sun's square with Chiron on January 6th may bring up past wounds or insecurities, but it also offers an opportunity for healing and growth. Use this time to address any emotional pain or self-doubt and seek support from loved ones or a professional if needed.

As the month progresses, the Sun's trine with Uranus on January 9th encourages you to embrace your unique qualities and express yourself authentically. You may experience a sudden surge of inspiration or a breakthrough moment that propels you forward.

In summary, January is a month of growth, transformation, and self-discovery for Aries. Embrace the challenges as opportunities for personal development and stay open to unexpected changes. With focus and determination, you can navigate this month with confidence and achieve remarkable progress.

## COMPLETE ARIES 2024 PERSONAL HOROSCOPE

Love:

Aries, your love life in January 2024 will be a mix of excitement, challenges, and growth. The astrological aspects influencing your romantic sphere require you to strike a balance between your personal desires and the needs of your partner.

At the beginning of the month, the Venus square Saturn aspect on January 1st may introduce some tension and obstacles in your relationship. This alignment encourages you to reassess your commitments and ensure that you and your partner are on the same page.

On January 3rd, Venus forms a quincunx aspect with Jupiter, highlighting the need for compromise and understanding. You may need to make adjustments to find a harmonious balance between your personal aspirations and the needs of your relationship.

Throughout January, Mars interacts with Pluto, Neptune, and Uranus, bringing intense and transformative energy to your love life. This energy can lead to passionate and profound experiences, but it may also bring unexpected changes or challenges.

The Sun's trine with Uranus on January 9th can bring exciting and liberating moments in your relationship. Embrace spontaneity and be open to trying new things together. This alignment can strengthen the bond between you and your partner and infuse your relationship with renewed vitality.

On January 15th, Venus squares Neptune, and you may need to be cautious of illusions or idealizations in your love life. It's essential to maintain realistic expectations and communicate openly with your partner to avoid misunderstandings.

Towards the end of the month, the Sun's square with Jupiter on January 27th can bring some conflict or differences of opinion. However, with open and honest communication, you can find resolutions and deepen your understanding of each other.

## Career:

Dear Aries, your professional life in January 2024 holds the promise of growth, opportunity, and transformative changes. The astrological aspects influencing your career sector encourage you to tap into your assertive and ambitious nature to achieve your goals.

At the beginning of the month, the Venus square Saturn aspect on January 1st may bring some challenges or delays in your career. However, this alignment also emphasizes the importance of discipline, patience, and long-term planning. Take this time to review your professional strategies and ensure that you are on the right path.

On January 3rd, Mercury's quintile with Saturn enhances your communication and organizational skills, allowing you to present your ideas and plans effectively. This alignment favors long-term planning, setting goals, and establishing solid foundations for future success.

Throughout January, Mars interacts with Pluto, Neptune, and Uranus, bringing a dynamic mix of energy and inspiration to your professional life. This combination can ignite your motivation, fuel your ambitions, and push you to take calculated risks.

The Sun's square with Chiron on January 6th may trigger some insecurities or past wounds related to your career. However, it also offers an opportunity for healing and growth. Use this time to address any self-doubt, seek support from mentors or colleagues, and embrace your inner strength.

The Sun's trine with Uranus on January 9th brings exciting opportunities for innovation and unconventional approaches to your work. Embrace your unique ideas and be open to new methods or technologies. Your ability to adapt quickly will help you stand out and advance in your career.

On January 27th, the Sun squares Jupiter, which can create some tensions or conflicts in your professional relationships. However, with diplomacy and a focus on collaboration, you can find solutions and create win-win situations.

### Finances:

Aries, in January 2024, the astrological aspects influencing your financial sector indicate a need for careful planning, realistic expectations, and adaptability. While there may be some challenges, there are also opportunities for growth and stability.

The month begins with Venus square Saturn on January 1st, which may introduce some financial obstacles or delays. This aspect reminds you to exercise caution and be mindful of your spending habits. Consider creating a budget and focusing on long-term financial goals to ensure stability.

On January 3rd, Venus forms a quincunx aspect with Jupiter, highlighting the need for balance between your desires and your financial responsibilities. It's essential to avoid impulsive purchases and find a harmonious approach that aligns your financial aspirations with practicality.

Throughout January, Mars interacts with Pluto, Neptune, and Uranus, bringing a mix of transformative energy, inspiration, and unexpected changes to your financial situation. This combination can bring both opportunities and challenges, requiring you to adapt quickly and make informed decisions.

The Sun's square with Chiron on January 6th may trigger some financial insecurities or past wounds. It's crucial to address any emotional issues related to money and develop a healthy relationship with your finances. Seek guidance from financial advisors or professionals if needed.

On January 9th, the Sun's trine with Uranus can bring unexpected financial opportunities or innovative ideas for increasing your income. Stay open to new possibilities and be willing to take calculated risks.

However, be cautious of Venus square Neptune on January 15th, as it may bring illusions or idealizations in your financial matters. Avoid making impulsive investments or trusting unreliable sources. Stick to practical and well-researched strategies to protect your financial well-being.

Health:

The month kicks off with Venus square Saturn on January 1st, which may bring some emotional challenges or feelings of heaviness. It's essential to take care of your emotional well-being by engaging in activities that bring you joy and seeking support from loved ones.

On January 3rd, Mercury's quintile with Saturn enhances your mental focus and clarity. Use this alignment to engage in mindfulness practices, meditation, or journaling. Taking time to nurture your mind will help you stay balanced and centered throughout the month.

Throughout January, Mars interacts with Pluto, Neptune, and Uranus, bringing a mix of transformative energy and inspiration to your physical vitality. This combination can enhance your motivation for physical activities and push you to explore new exercise routines or wellness practices.

The Sun's square with Chiron on January 6th may bring up old wounds or insecurities related to your health. Take this opportunity to address any underlying issues and seek professional advice if needed. Remember to practice self-compassion and focus on healing.

On January 15th, the Sun's sextile with Neptune encourages a holistic approach to your well-being. Explore alternative therapies, such as meditation, yoga, or energy healing, to enhance your overall health and restore balance in your life.

Throughout the month, prioritize proper nutrition, regular exercise, and sufficient rest. Nurturing your body and mind will provide you with the energy and vitality needed to navigate the month's challenges and seize the opportunities that come your way.

Remember to listen to your body and honor its needs. If you feel overwhelmed or fatigued, take time for self-care and relaxation. Embracing a healthy lifestyle and implementing stress-management techniques will contribute to your overall well-being.

## Travel

At the beginning of the month, the Venus square Saturn aspect on January 1st may introduce some obstacles or delays in your travel plans. However, this alignment encourages you to approach your travel arrangements with patience and flexibility. Consider having backup plans and be prepared for unexpected changes.

On January 9th, the Sun's trine with Uranus brings exciting and unexpected opportunities for travel. You may receive spontaneous invitations or discover new destinations that capture your interest. Embrace these opportunities and be open to exploring the unknown.

Throughout January, Mars interacts with Pluto, Neptune, and Uranus, infusing your travel experiences with transformative energy and inspiration. This combination can lead to profound and life-changing adventures. Be open to stepping out of your comfort zone and embracing new cultures, languages, and experiences.

However, be mindful of Venus square Neptune on January 15th, as it may create illusions or idealizations in your travel plans. Double-check details, read reviews, and ensure that your arrangements are reliable and trustworthy.

If you're planning business-related travel, the Sun's square with Jupiter on January 27th may bring some challenges or conflicts. Stay diplomatic and focused on finding solutions. Remember that these obstacles can also offer opportunities for personal and professional growth.

Insight from the Stars:

The universe is reminding you of the importance of patience and planning. While your fiery nature is one of your greatest strengths, this is a time to temper that fire with earthy practicality.

Best days of the month: January 9th, 15th, 19th, 23rd, 27th, 28th and 30th.

## February 2024

### Horoscope

Dear Aries, welcome to the transformative month of February 2024! This month brings a mix of opportunities, challenges, and profound shifts that will impact various aspects of your life. Embrace the transformative energy and use it to grow, evolve, and create positive change.

The month begins with Mars semi-square Saturn on February 2nd, which may bring some tension or obstacles in your path. However, this aspect also encourages you to face challenges head-on and persist in your pursuits.

On February 5th, the Sun's semi-sextile with Venus highlights the need for balance between your personal desires and your relationships. Strive to find harmony and compromise to maintain healthy connections.

Throughout February, Mars interacts with Pluto, Neptune, and Uranus, bringing transformative energy, inspiration, and unexpected changes. This combination intensifies your motivation, encourages you to explore new horizons, and provides opportunities for personal growth.

The Sun's conjunction with Pluto on February 5th empowers you to embrace your personal power and engage in deep self-reflection. Use this alignment to uncover your inner strength and transform any limiting beliefs or patterns.

On February 6th, the Sun's sextile with the True Node and Saturn's quintile with Uranus create a harmonious blend of stability and innovation. This alignment encourages you to embrace change while staying grounded and focused on long-term goals.

On February 19th, the True Node and Chiron conjunct in Aries, marking a significant moment of healing and soul growth. This alignment invites you to embrace vulnerability and utilize your experiences to inspire and guide others.

Throughout February, pay attention to your intuition and the subtle messages from the universe. Engage in spiritual practices, meditation, or journaling to deepen your connection with your inner self.

In summary, February is a month of transformation and growth for Aries. Embrace the powerful energy and use it to create positive changes in your life. Stay open to new opportunities, maintain healthy relationships, and trust in your own inner strength. By aligning with the cosmic forces, you can navigate the month with resilience, authenticity, and purpose.

## Love

Aries, February 2024 brings exciting and transformative energy to your love life. The astrological aspects influencing your romantic sector encourage you to embrace change, deepen your connections, and evolve in your relationships.

At the beginning of the month, the Sun's semi-sextile with Venus highlights the importance of balance in your relationships. Find a harmonious blend between your personal desires and the needs of your partner. Communication and compromise will be key to maintaining healthy connections.

Throughout February, Mars interacts with Pluto, Neptune, and Uranus, infusing your love life with intensity, passion, and unexpected shifts. This combination can bring profound changes and opportunities for growth in your romantic relationships.

On February 7th, Venus's trine with Uranus introduces excitement and spontaneity into your love life. Be open to new experiences and embrace the unexpected. This alignment can bring thrilling adventures and deepen the bond between you and your partner.

Throughout the month, Mercury's interactions with Chiron and the True Node create opportunities for healing and growth in your relationships. Honest and open communication will be essential to address any past wounds or misunderstandings.

The Sun's square with Uranus on February 8th may create some disruptions or conflicts in your love life. Stay calm and adaptable, and approach any challenges with a willingness to find solutions. This aspect can also lead to breakthrough moments that bring you closer to your partner.

On February 19th, the True Node and Chiron conjunct in Aries, offering a powerful opportunity for healing and growth in your relationships. Embrace vulnerability and let go of old patterns or limiting beliefs. This alignment can bring profound transformation and deepen the love and connection you share with your partner.

## Career

Aries, in February 2024, your career takes center stage as the astrological aspects bring opportunities for growth, professional development, and transformative changes. This month encourages you to assert yourself, take calculated risks, and embrace innovative approaches in your professional life.

At the beginning of the month, Mars semi-square Saturn on February 2nd may bring some tension or obstacles in your career path. However, this aspect also encourages you to face challenges with determination and persistence.

The Sun's semi-sextile with Venus on February 5th highlights the importance of balance in your professional relationships. Strive for harmonious interactions and seek cooperation and compromise to maintain a positive working environment.

Throughout February, Mars interacts with Pluto, Neptune, and Uranus, infusing your career sector with transformative energy and inspiration. This combination fuels your ambition, motivates you to take risks, and opens doors to new opportunities.

The Sun's conjunction with Pluto on February 5th empowers you to tap into your personal power and assertiveness. Use this alignment to delve deep into your ambitions and make significant changes in your professional life.

On February 6th, the Sun's sextile with the True Node and Saturn's quintile with Uranus create a harmonious blend of stability and innovation. This alignment encourages you to embrace change while staying grounded and focused on long-term goals.

Throughout the month, Mercury interacts with various planets, including Chiron and the True Node, enhancing your communication skills and bringing opportunities for professional growth. Engage in effective networking, express your ideas with confidence, and seek collaboration to advance your career.

The Sun's square with Uranus on February 8th may bring unexpected changes or disruptions in your professional life. Stay adaptable and open to new possibilities, as this aspect can also bring breakthrough moments and opportunities for personal and career advancement.

## Finance

Aries, in February 2024, your financial sector undergoes significant shifts and opportunities for growth. The astrological aspects influencing your finances encourage you to embrace change, take calculated risks, and exercise caution in your monetary decisions.

At the beginning of the month, Mars semi-square Saturn on February 2nd may bring some tension or obstacles in your financial matters. This aspect reminds you to approach financial challenges with patience and determination.

The Sun's semi-sextile with Venus on February 5th highlights the importance of balance in your financial decisions. Strive for a harmonious approach that aligns your desires with practicality. Avoid impulsive purchases and focus on long-term financial goals.

Throughout February, Mars interacts with Pluto, Neptune, and Uranus, infusing your financial sector with transformative energy and unexpected changes. This combination can bring both opportunities and challenges, requiring you to adapt quickly and make informed decisions.

The Sun's conjunction with Pluto on February 5th empowers you to transform your relationship with money. Use this alignment to uncover any limiting beliefs or patterns that may hinder your financial growth. Embrace a mindset of abundance and take steps to manifest your financial goals.

On February 7th, Venus's trine with Uranus introduces exciting and unexpected opportunities in your finances. Be open to new ventures or investment opportunities that come your way. However, exercise caution and do thorough research before committing to any financial decisions.

Throughout the month, pay attention to your financial intuition and trust your instincts. Engage in careful financial planning, track your expenses, and ensure that you have a solid budget in place.

The Sun's square with Uranus on February 8th may bring unexpected changes or disruptions in your financial situation. Stay adaptable and open-minded, as this aspect can also bring breakthrough moments and new avenues for financial growth.

## Health

At the beginning of the month, Mars semi-square Saturn on February 2nd may bring some tension or challenges to your overall well-being. This aspect reminds you to address any physical or mental imbalances and take proactive steps to maintain your health.

The Sun's semi-sextile with Venus on February 5th highlights the importance of balance and self-care. Strive for harmony between your physical, emotional, and mental well-being. Take time to engage in activities that nurture your body and bring you joy.

Throughout February, Mars interacts with Pluto, Neptune, and Uranus, infusing your health sector with transformative energy and inspiration. This combination can bring both challenges and opportunities for growth in your well-being.

The Sun's conjunction with Pluto on February 5th empowers you to delve deep into your physical and emotional health. Use this alignment to uncover any underlying issues and seek appropriate support and healing modalities.

On February 7th, Venus's trine with Uranus encourages you to explore new wellness practices and routines. Be open to alternative therapies, exercise regimens, or spiritual practices that resonate with you.

Throughout the month, pay attention to your intuition and listen to the subtle messages from your body. Engage in mindfulness practices, meditation, or journaling to enhance your self-awareness and connect with your inner self.

The Sun's square with Uranus on February 8th may bring unexpected disruptions or changes to your health routines. Stay adaptable and open to new approaches. This aspect can also lead to breakthrough moments and new insights into your well-being.

## Travel

At the beginning of the month, Mars semi-square Saturn on February 2nd may bring some tension or delays in your travel plans. This aspect reminds you to remain patient and flexible, as unexpected changes may arise.

The Sun's semi-sextile with Venus on February 5th highlights the importance of balance in your travel experiences. Seek harmony between exploration and relaxation, and allow yourself to savor the beauty of each destination.

Throughout February, Mars interacts with Pluto, Neptune, and Uranus, infusing your travel adventures with transformative energy and inspiration. This combination can bring both excitement and unexpected changes to your journeys.

The Sun's conjunction with Pluto on February 5th empowers you to embrace the transformative power of travel. Use this alignment to explore new cultures, expand your horizons, and gain a deeper understanding of the world around you.

On February 7th, Venus's trine with Uranus introduces opportunities for spontaneous and thrilling adventures. Be open to unexpected opportunities and embrace the joy of exploration.

Throughout the month, trust your intuition when planning your travel experiences. Engage in research, read reviews, and be open to serendipitous encounters along the way.

The Sun's square with Uranus on February 8th may bring unexpected changes or disruptions in your travel plans. Stay adaptable and open-minded, as this aspect can also lead to exciting and memorable experiences.

## COMPLETE ARIES 2024 PERSONAL HOROSCOPE

### Insights from the stars

This month, the universe reminds you that life is a delicate dance of giving and receiving, action and reflection. Embrace the dance with an open heart and a grounded spirit.

Best days of the month: February 7th, 15th, 19th, 22nd, 27th, 28th and 29th.

## March 2024

### Horoscope

Dear Aries, March 2024 brings a dynamic and transformative energy to your life. The astrological aspects influencing your sign encourage growth, self-discovery, and courageous action. It's a month of embracing change, deepening relationships, and aligning with your true purpose.

At the beginning of the month, the Sun's sextile with Jupiter on March 1st infuses you with optimism, confidence, and a sense of expansion. This alignment empowers you to pursue your dreams and take calculated risks to achieve your goals.

Throughout March, Mercury, the planet of communication, interacts with various celestial bodies, amplifying your mental agility and creativity. On March 2nd, Mercury's semi-sextile with Mars enhances your ability to express your ideas assertively and take decisive action. Use this energy to pursue your passions and assert yourself in all areas of life.

On March 3rd, Venus squares Uranus, bringing a touch of unpredictability to your love life and relationships. This aspect encourages you to embrace change and be open to unconventional connections and experiences. However, be mindful of impulsive actions and seek balance in your interactions.

The Sun's semi-sextile with Pluto on March 6th empowers you to tap into your personal power and transform any aspects of your life that no longer serve you. Use this alignment to release old patterns and embrace a renewed sense of self.

Throughout the month, Mars, your ruling planet, interacts with Neptune and Chiron, infusing your actions with compassion, spiritual insight, and healing energy. Embrace your intuitive nature and trust your instincts as you navigate through various situations.

On March 18th, Mercury's conjunction with the True Node enhances your ability to connect with others on a deep, soul level. This alignment brings opportunities for meaningful conversations, profound connections, and collaboration.

The Sun's sextile with Pluto on March 21st further empowers you to harness your inner strength and make transformative changes in your life. This aspect encourages you to embrace your true identity and pursue your passions with unwavering determination.

March 2024 invites you to step into your authentic self, embrace change, and take bold actions. Trust your instincts, nurture your relationships, and explore new horizons. This is a month of personal growth, empowerment, and deepening connections.

## Love

In March 2024, Aries, love takes center stage in your life. The celestial aspects influencing your love sector bring opportunities for deepening connections, exploring new experiences, and finding harmony in your relationships.

The square between Venus and Uranus on March 3rd introduces an element of excitement and unpredictability in your love life. Be open to unexpected changes and new connections that may challenge your preconceived notions of love. Embrace the potential for growth and adventure.

Throughout the month, Venus interacts with Neptune and Chiron, infusing your love experiences with compassion, spiritual connection, and healing energy. This combination encourages you to prioritize emotional intimacy, trust, and vulnerability in your relationships.

On March 6th, Venus's semi-sextile with Pluto invites you to delve into the depths of your emotions and transform any outdated patterns that hinder your ability to experience love fully. Embrace your inner power and release any fears or insecurities that may hold you back.

The Sun's semi-sextile with Chiron on March 7th further supports your journey of healing and self-discovery in relationships. This aspect encourages you to be authentic, communicate your needs, and embrace vulnerability with your loved ones.

March 18th marks a significant day for deep connections and soulful interactions as Mercury conjoins the True Node. This alignment brings opportunities for heartfelt conversations and meaningful connections. It's a time to open up, share your true self, and listen to others with empathy and understanding.

## Career

In March 2024, Aries, the astrological influences bring a dynamic energy to your career and professional pursuits. This is a month of expansion, innovation, and assertive action in your work life.

Mercury's interactions with Mars and Jupiter throughout the month amplify your communication skills, mental agility, and confidence. On March 2nd, Mercury's semi-sextile with Mars empowers you to express your ideas assertively and take decisive action. Use this energy to pursue new projects, present your ideas to superiors, or take on leadership roles.

On March 18th, Mercury's conjunction with the True Node enhances your ability to connect with others on a deep, soul level. This alignment is favorable for collaborative efforts, networking, and building meaningful professional relationships. Embrace teamwork and seek opportunities for mutual growth and support.

The Sun's sextile with Pluto on March 21st brings a transformative energy to your career path. This aspect empowers you to tap into your personal power, make influential changes, and assert yourself confidently in your professional endeavors. Embrace your inner strength and pursue your goals with determination.

Throughout the month, Mars interacts with Neptune and Chiron, infusing your actions with compassion, spiritual insight, and healing energy. This combination encourages you to align your work with your higher purpose, find meaning in your endeavors, and contribute to the well-being of others.

## Finance

In March 2024, Aries, the celestial aspects influencing your financial sector invite you to take a mindful and strategic approach to your finances. This is a month of balancing your expenses, making thoughtful investments, and aligning your financial goals with your values.

The square between Venus and Uranus on March 3rd may bring some unexpected financial changes or expenses. It's important to be adaptable and open to alternative solutions to any financial challenges that arise. Embrace a flexible mindset and seek opportunities for innovative approaches to your finances.

Throughout the month, Venus interacts with Neptune and Chiron, infusing your financial decisions with compassion, spiritual awareness, and a focus on long-term sustainability. This combination encourages you to align your financial pursuits with your values, seek investments that support your personal growth, and prioritize financial well-being.

On March 12th, Venus's semi-sextile with Pluto invites you to reflect on your relationship with money and transform any outdated beliefs or patterns that hinder your financial growth. Embrace an empowered mindset and release any fears or scarcity mentality.

The Sun's semi-square with Jupiter on March 19th encourages you to find a balance between optimism and practicality in your financial decisions. Avoid overextending yourself or taking unnecessary risks.

Instead, seek stability and make decisions based on careful analysis and long-term benefits.

## Health

Mars, your ruling planet, interacts with Neptune and Chiron throughout the month, infusing your actions and energy with compassion, spiritual insight, and healing energy. This combination encourages you to listen to your body's needs, honor your emotions, and seek holistic approaches to your well-being.

Pay attention to your energy levels and avoid pushing yourself too hard. Practice mindful movement, such as yoga or meditation, to balance your physical and mental state. Nurture your emotional well-being through journaling, therapy, or connecting with loved ones.

On March 7th, the Sun's semi-sextile with Chiron supports your healing journey and encourages you to embrace vulnerability in addressing any health issues.

Seek professional advice, listen to your body's wisdom, and be proactive in taking care of your well-being.

## Travel

Whether it's a short getaway or a long-distance adventure, this month encourages you to embrace new experiences, expand your horizons, and indulge in your sense of adventure.

The square between Venus and Uranus on March 3rd may introduce some unexpected twists or changes to your travel plans. Embrace a flexible mindset and be open to alternative destinations or itineraries. Spontaneity may lead to exciting and unique experiences.

As Mars interacts with Neptune and Chiron throughout the month, your travel experiences are infused with compassion, spiritual insight, and healing energy. Embrace a mindful and present approach to your journeys, allowing yourself to be fully immersed in the beauty and wonder of new environments.

On March 19th, the Sun's sextile with Jupiter amplifies your sense of adventure and encourages you to expand your horizons. This aspect brings opportunities for growth, cultural exploration, and meaningful connections with people from different backgrounds.

When planning your travels, consider destinations that offer a blend of adventure, relaxation, and opportunities for personal growth. Seek experiences that align with your interests and values, whether it's immersing yourself in nature, exploring historical sites, or engaging with local communities.

Embrace a spirit of spontaneity and be open to unexpected opportunities that may arise during your travels. Allow yourself to step out of your comfort zone, try new activities, and embrace the unknown. Each experience has the potential to expand your perspective and enrich your soul.

Insights from the stars

March is a month of beginnings for Aries. The stars beckon you to embrace your inner warrior and forge ahead, but with wisdom and balance. Your ruling planet reminds you of the importance of structure and discipline in achieving your goals.

Best days of the month: March 1st, 7th, 12th, 18th, 19th, 21st and 25th.

## April 2024

### Horoscope

Dear Aries, April 2024 is a month of self-discovery and personal growth. With the Sun in your sign for the majority of the month, your energy levels are high, and your personality shines brightly. This is an ideal time to focus on personal development, setting new goals, and taking steps toward fulfilling your dreams. The cosmos encourages you to embrace your unique qualities and live authentically.

April 2024 is a dynamic and transformative month for Aries. The energies are ripe for personal growth, romantic endeavors, career advancements, and exciting journeys. Embrace the vitality of April and harness it to mold your destiny. Let your spirit be bold, your heart be open, and your actions be wise.

### Love

This month is marked by a powerful blend of passion, drive, and introspection. It's a time for self-discovery, personal growth, and embracing the changes that come your way.

The month begins with the Sun's semi-sextile with Saturn on April 2nd, encouraging you to find a balance between assertiveness and patience. Take time to assess your goals and make practical plans to achieve them. This aspect also reminds you to be mindful of your responsibilities and commitments.

The Sun's quintile with Pluto on April 3rd deepens your self-awareness and empowers you to tap into your inner strength and resilience. Use this energy to transform any areas of your life that are in need of change or improvement. Trust in your ability to overcome challenges and embrace your personal power.

Mars quintile Uranus on April 3rd ignites your adventurous spirit and fuels your desire for freedom and excitement. You may feel a strong urge to break free from routine and embrace new experiences. Allow yourself to explore uncharted territory and seize opportunities that align with your passions.

Venus's conjunction with Neptune on April 3rd brings a touch of romance, creativity, and dreaminess to your love life. This aspect encourages you to express your emotions and connect with others on a deeper, more compassionate level. It's a favorable time for romantic gestures, artistic pursuits, and nurturing your relationships.

The Sun's conjunction with the True Node on April 4th amplifies your sense of purpose and destiny.

This alignment invites you to step into your authentic self and align your actions with your soul's calling. Trust in the path that unfolds before you and embrace the opportunities for growth and self-discovery.

## Career

The Sun's semi-sextile with Jupiter on April 8th expands your horizons and opens doors to new possibilities in your career. This aspect encourages you to step out of your comfort zone, embrace challenges, and seek opportunities for advancement. Trust in your abilities and have faith in your potential.

Venus's semi-square with Jupiter on April 8th may introduce some tensions or conflicts in your professional relationships. Be mindful of any power struggles or clashes of ego that may arise. Focus on diplomacy and finding a harmonious balance between asserting yourself and collaborating with others.

The Sun's conjunction with Mercury on April 11th enhances your communication skills and intellectual prowess in your professional endeavors. This alignment supports productive discussions, negotiations, and problem-solving. It's a favorable time to present your ideas, network with influential individuals, and make progress in your career.

## Finance

In April 2024, Aries, the astrological influences bring a mix of opportunities and challenges to your financial landscape. This month requires careful consideration of your spending habits and a balanced approach to money matters.

Venus's semi-square with Uranus on April 10th may bring unexpected financial changes or expenses. It's important to be prepared for the unexpected and have a contingency plan in place. Avoid impulsive purchases and assess the long-term impact of your financial decisions.

The Sun's semi-sextile with Neptune on April 17th calls for financial discernment and wise judgment. Be cautious of potential scams or deceptive financial offers. Trust your intuition and seek professional advice if needed. Focus on maintaining financial stability and protecting your assets.

## Health

In April 2024, Aries, the astrological influences remind you to prioritize your health and well-being. This month calls for self-care, balance, and nurturing your mind, body, and soul.

The Sun's conjunction with Chiron on April 8th brings healing energy to your physical and emotional well-being. This aspect invites you to address any lingering health issues or emotional wounds. Seek holistic approaches to healing and incorporate self-care practices that support your overall well-being.

Mercury's semi-sextile with Saturn on April 24th emphasizes the importance of mental and emotional stability. Pay attention to your thought patterns and seek healthy outlets for stress management. Find ways to maintain a healthy work-life balance and prioritize relaxation and rejuvenation.

## Travel

This month offers opportunities for exciting journeys, both physical and metaphorical.

Venus's semi-sextile with Mars on April 6th brings a sense of adventure and spontaneity to your travel plans. It's an excellent time to embark on a spontaneous trip or engage in outdoor activities that invigorate your spirit. Embrace new experiences and expand your horizons through travel.

The Sun's square with Pluto on April 21st invites you to explore the depths of your own psyche and embark on a journey of self-discovery. This may involve inner travel, introspection, and engaging in transformative practices such as meditation or spiritual retreats. Allow yourself to delve into the depths of your soul and embrace the transformative power of self-exploration.

Insights from the stars

April is a power-packed month for Aries. The stars are aligned in a way that enhances your natural qualities of leadership, courage, and enthusiasm. However, with great power comes great responsibility. The stars remind you to wield your energies wisely.

Best days of the month: April 3rd, 8th, 11th, 17th, 19th, 20th, and 24th.

## May 2024

### Horoscope

The astrological influences encourage you to embrace change, explore new opportunities, and cultivate a deeper understanding of yourself and your relationships. This month presents a blend of challenges and growth, offering you the chance to evolve and manifest your desires.

The square between Venus and Pluto on May 1st may bring intense emotional experiences in your relationships. It's essential to maintain open communication, trust, and honesty to navigate any power struggles or control issues. Use this opportunity to transform and strengthen your connections through deep emotional healing.

Mars's sextile with Pluto on May 3rd empowers you with a potent drive and determination to pursue your goals. Your assertiveness and ambition are heightened, and you possess the ability to overcome obstacles and make significant progress in your endeavors. Embrace this transformative energy to create positive change in your life.

## Love

The planetary alignments invite you to delve deeper into your relationships, fostering emotional connections and strengthening the bonds you share. The semi-square between Venus and Neptune on May 10th may bring moments of confusion or uncertainty in your romantic partnerships. It's crucial to maintain clarity and open communication to navigate any misunderstandings or illusions. Trust your intuition and take time to connect with your emotions and desires.

The Sun's semi-sextile with Chiron on May 11th presents an opportunity for emotional healing and growth in your love life. This aspect invites you to address any emotional wounds or insecurities that may be impacting your relationships. Vulnerability and open-heartedness allow for deeper intimacy and connection.

## Career

In May 2024, Aries, the astrological influences highlight your professional ambitions and bring opportunities for advancement and recognition. This month presents a favorable period to pursue your career goals and make significant strides in your chosen field.

Mercury's conjunction with Chiron on May 6th enhances your communication skills and allows for healing conversations in the workplace. It's an excellent time to address any conflicts or misunderstandings and find resolutions that promote harmony and productivity. Use your words wisely and express your ideas with confidence and compassion.

The Sun's conjunction with Uranus on May 13th brings unexpected opportunities and innovative ideas in your career. Embrace change and be open to new approaches and perspectives. This alignment encourages you to think outside the box and take calculated risks that can lead to breakthroughs and success.

## Finance

In May 2024, Aries, the astrological influences in the realm of finances bring a need for cautiousness and practicality. It's essential to make informed decisions and avoid impulsive spending or risky investments.

Venus's semi-square with Mars on May 10th may create financial tension or conflicting desires. It's important to find a balance between enjoying the pleasures of life and maintaining financial stability. Be mindful of your spending habits and prioritize long-term financial goals.

The Sun's conjunction with Jupiter on May 18th brings opportunities for financial expansion and abundance. This aspect favors strategic planning, investments, and the pursuit of new income streams. Take advantage of favorable financial opportunities that come your way, but ensure they align with your long-term goals and values.

## Health

In May 2024, Aries, the astrological influences highlight the importance of self-care and maintaining a balanced approach to your health and well-being. It's crucial to prioritize self-care routines and create a harmonious balance between work and rest.

The Sun's semi-square with Chiron on May 27th may bring some emotional and physical sensitivity. Take time to nurture yourself and address any underlying emotional wounds or stressors. Engage in activities that bring you joy and relaxation, such as exercise, meditation, or spending time in nature.

Pay attention to your energy levels and listen to your body's needs. Establish healthy boundaries and avoid overexertion or burnout. Remember that self-care is a vital component of overall well-being, and taking care of yourself enables you to show up fully in other areas of your life.

## Travel

It's a favorable time to expand your horizons and embark on new journeys.

Planetary alignments encourage spontaneity and embracing the unknown. Allow yourself to step out of your comfort zone and explore new destinations or engage in unique experiences. Traveling can provide valuable insights, broaden your perspective, and offer opportunities for personal growth.

When planning your trips, ensure you have a flexible itinerary to accommodate any unexpected changes or delays. Embrace the sense of adventure and be open to connecting with people from different cultures and backgrounds. These interactions can bring valuable insights and broaden your understanding of the world.

## Insights from the stars

The stars in May whisper of growth and change. This is the time to set intentions, particularly regarding relationships and personal values.

Best days of the month: May 7th, 13th, 18th, 19th, 23rd, 25th and 30th.

# June 2024

## Horoscope

In June 2024, Aries, the astrological influences bring a combination of dynamism, intuition, and emotional growth. This month offers opportunities for personal transformation and deepening your connections with others. It's a time to trust your instincts and embrace your authentic self.

Mars's semi-sextile with Uranus on June 1st ignites your desire for freedom and independence. This aspect encourages you to break free from limitations and explore new possibilities. Embrace your unique individuality and allow your innovative ideas to flourish.

The Sun's quintile with Neptune on June 1st enhances your intuition and spiritual connection. Trust your inner guidance and pay attention to subtle signs and synchronicities. Engaging in practices such as meditation and journaling can help deepen your spiritual connection and enhance your overall well-being.

## Love

In June 2024, Aries, the astrological influences in the realm of love and relationships bring opportunities for growth, passion, and deep emotional connections.

It's a time to explore the depths of your heart and nurture the bonds you have with your loved ones.

Venus's sextile with Chiron on June 11th promotes healing and emotional growth in your relationships. It's a favorable aspect for addressing any past wounds or emotional barriers that may have been hindering your connection. Open up to vulnerability and allow yourself to receive and give love freely.

The Sun's conjunction with Venus on June 4th amplifies your charm and attractiveness. This alignment enhances your romantic energy and may bring new opportunities for love or deepen existing relationships. Embrace the beauty of love and let your heart guide you in matters of the heart.

## Career

This month presents opportunities for growth, recognition, and the manifestation of your ambitions. It's a time to assert yourself and make strides towards your goals.

Mercury's conjunction with Jupiter on June 4th enhances your communication skills and intellectual prowess. This alignment supports your ability to convey your ideas effectively and make persuasive arguments. It's a favorable time for negotiations, presentations, or any endeavors that require clear and compelling communication.

The Sun's square with Saturn on June 9th may bring some challenges or obstacles in your career. It's important to stay persistent and focused on your long-term goals. Use this aspect as an opportunity to reassess your plans, strengthen your strategies, and approach your work with discipline and dedication.

## Finance

In June 2024, Aries, the astrological influences in the realm of finances emphasize the importance of stability, discipline, and wise financial decisions. It's a time to evaluate your financial goals, manage your resources effectively, and make informed choices.

Venus's square with Saturn on June 8th may bring some financial challenges or restrictions. It's essential to create a solid budget and exercise caution in your spending habits. Focus on long-term financial security and avoid impulsive purchases or risky investments.

The Sun's quincunx with Pluto on June 22nd calls for a reevaluation of your financial strategies and power dynamics. Reflect on any hidden patterns or beliefs that may be influencing your relationship with money. Embrace financial empowerment and make choices that align with your values and long-term goals.

## Health

In June 2024, Aries, the astrological influences highlight the importance of self-care, emotional well-being, and maintaining a balanced approach to your health. It's essential to prioritize self-care routines and nurture your mind, body, and spirit.

The Sun's quintile with Chiron on June 26th supports your emotional healing and self-discovery journey. Take time for introspection and self-reflection. Engage in activities that bring you joy, such as exercise, meditation, or creative outlets. Connect with your emotions and seek support when needed.

Maintain a balanced approach to your physical health. Focus on nourishing foods, regular exercise, and adequate rest. Listen to your body's needs and establish healthy boundaries to avoid overexertion or burnout.

## Travel

Mars's semi-sextile with Jupiter on June 15th ignites your adventurous spirit and encourages you to embark on exciting journeys. Whether it's a spontaneous weekend getaway or a carefully planned international trip, embrace the spirit of adventure and allow yourself to be open to new experiences. Pay attention to any travel-related restrictions or guidelines and plan accordingly. Research your destinations, connect with locals, and immerse yourself in different cultures. These experiences will not only provide joy and relaxation but also expand your understanding of the world.

## Insights from the stars

The stars in June are aligned to foster intellectual growth and emotional nurturing for Aries. Listen to your intuition this month as it will guide you through the changing tides. Remember that balancing the mind and heart is crucial. The stars offer you the energies, but it is your conscious choices that will shape your path.

Best days of the month: June 14th, 16th, 20th, 21st, 22nd, 26th, and 29th.

## July 2024

### Horoscope

This month encourages you to embrace change, pursue personal growth, and explore new possibilities. It's a time to tap into your inner power, assert your individuality, and make significant strides towards your goals.

Jupiter's semi-square with Chiron on July 1st invites you to confront any emotional wounds and seek healing. Take the time to address any unresolved issues and prioritize self-care. Trust the process of healing, and remember that vulnerability is a strength.

Mercury's quintile with Mars on July 1st enhances your mental agility and assertiveness. This aspect supports effective communication and empowers you to express your ideas and opinions with confidence. Use this energy to pursue your goals and assert yourself in professional and personal interactions.

The Sun's semi-square with Uranus on July 1st brings unexpected events and changes to your daily routine. Embrace the element of surprise and be open to adapting to new circumstances. It's through these unexpected experiences that you'll discover hidden opportunities for growth.

## Love

In July 2024, Aries, the astrological influences bring passion and intensity to your love life. This month encourages you to be bold in expressing your desires and nurturing your relationships.

Mercury's opposition with Pluto on July 3rd may bring intense conversations and the need for emotional depth in your partnerships. Dive beneath the surface and engage in honest and transformative discussions. Use this energy to strengthen your emotional bonds and create a deeper understanding with your partner.

Venus's square with Chiron on July 6th calls for healing and compassion in matters of the heart. This aspect may bring up past wounds or insecurities. Be patient with yourself and your partner as you navigate through these emotions. Offer support and understanding and allow space for emotional healing to take place.

## Career

This month offers opportunities for advancement, recognition, and the manifestation of your ambitions.

It's a time to assert your leadership skills, showcase your talents, and make significant progress in your chosen field.

Venus's trine with Saturn on July 2nd brings stability and practicality to your career. This aspect supports long-term planning and disciplined efforts. Use this influence to establish a solid foundation, build professional relationships, and make wise decisions that contribute to your long-term success.

Mercury's sextile with Jupiter on July 8th enhances your communication skills and expands your network. This alignment fosters positive interactions, collaboration, and sharing of ideas. Use this influence to connect with influential individuals, seek mentorship, and explore new opportunities for growth and development.

## Finance

In July 2024, Aries, the astrological influences encourage you to pay attention to your financial stability and long-term goals. This month calls for practicality and disciplined money management.

Mercury's quincunx with Saturn on July 15th invites you to evaluate your financial habits and make adjustments if necessary. Assess your budget, cut unnecessary expenses, and focus on long-term investments that align with your financial goals.

Venus's trine with Neptune on July 11th brings an opportunity for intuitive financial decision-making. Trust your instincts when it comes to financial matters and seek out opportunities that align with your values. Avoid impulsive spending and make choices that contribute to your long-term financial well-being.

### Health

This month encourages you to maintain a balance between physical activity, rest, and self-care.

Mars's conjunction with Uranus on July 15th energizes your physical body and encourages you to explore new forms of exercise and movement. Embrace activities that challenge and excite you, such as trying a new sport or engaging in high-intensity workouts. However, remember to listen to your body and avoid pushing yourself beyond your limits.

The Sun's trine with Neptune on July 21st invites you to find harmony and balance through relaxation and self-reflection. Take time to rest and recharge, engage in activities that promote inner peace and emotional well-being, such as meditation, yoga, or spending time in nature. Listen to your intuition and honor your body's signals.

## Travel

This month invites you to broaden your horizons, experience new cultures, and create lasting memories. Venus's quintile with Uranus on July 8th ignites your adventurous spirit and encourages you to embark on exciting journeys. Whether it's a spontaneous weekend getaway or a carefully planned international trip, embrace the spirit of adventure and allow yourself to be open to new experiences.

Pay attention to any travel-related restrictions or guidelines and plan accordingly. Research your destinations, connect with locals, and immerse yourself in different cultures. These experiences will not only provide joy and relaxation but also expand your understanding of the world.

## Insights from the stars

This month the stars urges Aries to nurture their emotional world, harmonize their domestic life, and express their unique self. Embrace the energies of the month with an open heart and let the stars guide your journey.

Best days of the month: July 10th, 15th, 18th, 21st, 23rd, 26th and 31st.

## August 2024

### Horoscope

In August 2024, Aries, the astrological influences bring a mix of energy and opportunities for self-reflection. This month encourages you to find a balance between taking action and introspection. It's a time to assess your goals, relationships, and personal growth, and make any necessary adjustments to align with your true desires.

Mars's sextile with True Node on August 1st ignites your motivation and drives you towards your goals. This aspect empowers you to take decisive actions that contribute to your personal and professional development. Trust your instincts and embrace opportunities that align with your authentic self.

Venus's square with Uranus on August 2nd may bring unexpected changes or disruptions in your love life and relationships. It's essential to remain adaptable and open-minded during this time. Embrace spontaneity and allow room for growth and evolution in your partnerships.

The Sun's biquintile with Saturn on August 4th supports your disciplined approach to work and personal responsibilities. This alignment enhances your ability to structure your time effectively, set goals, and make steady progress. Embrace the rewards of hard work and perseverance.

## Love

This month invites you to deepen your connections, express your desires, and foster emotional intimacy.

Venus's quintile with Jupiter on August 2nd enhances your romantic nature and expands your capacity for joy and love. This aspect encourages you to embrace positive experiences and create opportunities for growth and adventure in your relationships.

Pay attention to Venus's square with Mars on August 22nd, as it may bring some tension or conflicts in your love life. Use this energy as an opportunity for honest communication and understanding. Seek compromise and find common ground with your partner to maintain harmony.

## Career

In August 2024, Aries, the astrological influences highlight your career and professional endeavors. This month presents opportunities for growth, recognition, and advancement. It's a time to assert your leadership skills, pursue your ambitions, and make significant strides in your chosen field.

Mars's conjunction with Jupiter on August 14th amplifies your drive and ambition. This aspect inspires you to take bold actions, explore new possibilities, and expand your professional horizons. Embrace opportunities for growth and trust your abilities to succeed.

Mercury's square with Uranus on August 18th brings an innovative and unconventional energy to your career. This aspect encourages you to think outside the box, embrace change, and take calculated risks. Trust your instincts and be open to new ideas and perspectives that can lead to breakthroughs in your professional life.

## Finance

Venus's opposition with Neptune on August 28th cautions you to be cautious when it comes to financial decisions. Avoid impulsive spending or risky investments during this time. Take a step back and assess your financial situation with clarity and objectivity.

Focus on Venus's trine with Pluto on August 29th, which brings opportunities for financial transformation and empowerment. This aspect supports strategic planning, long-term investments, and exploring ways to increase your financial abundance. Seek advice from professionals and take proactive steps to secure your financial future.

### Health

This month calls for a balance between taking care of your body and nurturing your inner self.

Mars's quintile with Neptune on August 6th encourages you to explore holistic approaches to health and wellness. Consider incorporating practices like meditation, yoga, or energy healing into your routine. Focus on self-care and stress management techniques to maintain optimal health.

Pay attention to the Sun's sesquiquadrate with Chiron on August 30th, as it may bring up emotional wounds or vulnerabilities. Take the time to address any lingering issues and seek support from trusted friends or professionals. Emotional healing is an essential aspect of overall well-being.

## Travel

Venus's trine with Uranus on August 27th sparks your sense of adventure and encourages you to embark on exciting journeys. Whether it's a spontaneous weekend getaway or a carefully planned international trip, embrace the spirit of exploration and embrace new experiences.

Pay attention to any travel restrictions or guidelines and plan accordingly. Research your destinations, connect with locals, and engage in activities that resonate with your sense of adventure. Embrace the opportunities for personal growth and cultural enrichment that travel brings.

## Insights from the stars

August is a month of duality for Aries – beginning with creative expression and ending with practicality. Balance is key; enjoy the playfulness of Leo and the diligence of Virgo.

Best days of the month: August $6^{th}$, $14^{th}$, $15^{th}$, $18^{th}$, $22^{nd}$, $27^{th}$ and $30^{th}$.

## September 2024

### Horoscope

In September 2024, Aries, the astrological influences bring a mix of introspection and assertiveness. This month encourages you to find a balance between reflection and taking action. It's a time to delve deep into your inner world, reassess your relationships, and embrace opportunities for personal and professional growth.

Mercury's trine with Chiron on September 2nd invites introspection and healing. This aspect supports deep conversations and self-reflection, allowing you to address emotional wounds and find inner peace. Take the time to communicate your feelings and seek understanding in your relationships.

Pay attention to the Sun's quintile with Mars on September 2nd, which enhances your motivation and assertiveness. This aspect empowers you to take bold actions and pursue your goals with vigor. Trust your instincts and embrace opportunities for growth and advancement.

## Love

In September 2024, Aries, the astrological influences bring a focus on your love life and relationships. This month encourages you to nurture your connections, express your emotions, and deepen your bonds.

Venus's opposition with the True Node on September 3rd may bring some challenges or conflicts in your relationships. It's essential to communicate openly and honestly with your partner, seeking a balance between your needs and theirs. Embrace compromise and find common ground to maintain harmony.

Pay attention to Venus's quincunx with Chiron on September 16th, as it may bring up insecurities or emotional vulnerabilities. Use this energy as an opportunity for growth and healing. Practice self-love and cultivate open communication with your partner to strengthen your bond.

## Career

In September 2024, Aries, the astrological influences highlight your career and professional aspirations. This month presents opportunities for growth, innovation, and collaboration. It's a time to assert your leadership skills and embrace new challenges.

Mars's quintile with Chiron on September 12th sparks your creativity and encourages you to find innovative solutions to work-related issues. This aspect empowers you to think outside the box and make significant strides in your professional endeavors. Trust your instincts and take calculated risks.

Pay attention to Mercury's biquintile with Pluto on September 12th, which brings transformative energy to your career. This aspect supports strategic planning and helps you gain insights into your professional path. Embrace the power of knowledge and make use of your communication skills to make an impact in your field.

Finance

Venus's biquintile with Uranus on September 15th sparks opportunities for financial innovation and unexpected gains. Embrace new investment strategies or explore alternative sources of income. Stay open to unique opportunities that can bring financial abundance.

Pay attention to Venus's quincunx with Saturn on September 29th, as it may bring some financial challenges or restrictions. It's essential to prioritize financial planning, budgeting, and responsible decision-making. Seek advice from professionals if needed and make thoughtful choices to ensure long-term financial stability.

### Health

The Sun's trine with Uranus on September 19th brings an energetic boost and encourages you to explore new approaches to health and wellness. Embrace innovative exercise routines or try alternative healing modalities to support your overall well-being.

Pay attention to the Sun's opposition with Neptune on September 20th, as it may bring some emotional sensitivity or confusion. Take time for self-reflection and ensure you're taking care of your mental and emotional health. Engage in activities that bring you joy and practice mindfulness to maintain inner balance.

### Travel

Venus's trine with Jupiter on September 15th sparks your sense of adventure and encourages you to embark on exciting journeys. Whether it's a spontaneous weekend getaway or a well-planned international trip, embrace the spirit of exploration and immerse yourself in new experiences.

Pay attention to the Sun's opposition with the True Node on September 29th, as it may bring some unexpected changes or delays in your travel plans. Be adaptable and flexible, and have contingency plans in place. Embrace the opportunities for personal growth and cultural enrichment that travel offers.

Insights from the stars

September is a month of organization, relationships, and unexpected events for Aries. The Virgo energy encourages practicality, while Libra focuses on balance in relationships. Uranus brings surprises, so be adaptable. Focus on clarity in communication and building strong relationships, both personally and professionally.

Best days of the month: September 2nd, 12th, 15th, 19th, 20th, 29th and 30th.

## October 2024

### Horoscope

Dear Aries, October 2024 brings a mix of energetic and transformative influences for you. It's a month of self-discovery, growth, and deep reflection. The planetary alignments invite you to embrace change, assert your boundaries, and focus on personal development. It's a time to let go of old patterns and make space for new beginnings. Stay open-minded and adaptable as you navigate the dynamic energy of this month. Trust in your ability to handle whatever comes your way and remember that transformation often leads to growth and positive outcomes. Embrace this opportunity for self-transformation and align your actions with your true desires and values. Use this month to establish a solid foundation for your future endeavors and cultivate harmonious relationships.

## Love

In love, Aries, October 2024 holds the potential for deep emotional connections and transformative experiences. The alignment of Venus and the True Node on October 3rd enhances your ability to form meaningful and soulful connections. You may be drawn to partners who have a significant impact on your life path and spiritual growth. This alignment invites you to open your heart and embrace vulnerability, allowing for profound and authentic connections.

On October 4th, Venus forms a trine with Saturn, bringing stability and commitment to your relationships. If you're in a committed partnership, this is a favorable time to solidify your bond, express your love and devotion, and work through any challenges together. Single Aries may attract someone who is mature, reliable, and ready for a committed relationship. The energy of this aspect supports building long-lasting foundations based on trust and shared values.

However, it's important to be mindful of the potential emotional wounds that may surface. Mercury's opposition with Chiron on October 8th can bring up insecurities and past hurts in relationships. This is an opportunity for healing and understanding. Engage in open and honest communication with your partner, addressing any emotional issues that arise. Seek support from trusted friends, family, or professionals if needed.

Overall, October presents an opportunity for profound emotional growth and transformation in your love life. Embrace vulnerability, communicate authentically, and foster connections that align with your deepest desires. Remember that true love requires effort, commitment, and a willingness to grow together.

## Career

In terms of your career, Aries, October 2024 holds potential for growth, collaboration, and assertiveness. The square between Mercury and Mars on October 6th may temporarily cloud your vision or create confusion regarding your professional goals. Take this opportunity to reassess your plans, ensuring they align with your authentic desires and values. Seek clarity before moving forward.

A significant aspect occurs on October 15th when Venus forms a trine with Mars. This alignment enhances your charisma and attracts positive attention in your career. It's an excellent time to showcase your skills, present new ideas, or launch creative projects.

Collaboration and cooperation with colleagues can lead to significant advancements. Leverage your ability to work well with others and inspire them with your enthusiasm and vision.

The Sun's quincunx with Uranus on October 19th may bring unexpected changes or disruptions in your career path. Stay adaptable and open to new opportunities that may arise. Trust in your ability to handle whatever comes your way and maintain a flexible mindset.

On October 21st, Mercury's biquintile with the True Node highlights the importance of aligning your career choices with your life path and purpose. This alignment encourages you to follow your intuition and make decisions that resonate with your soul's journey. Trust that the universe will guide you towards fulfilling professional experiences.

## Finances

The sesquiquadrate aspect between Venus and Neptune on October 3rd may bring some confusion or idealistic tendencies regarding your financial situation. It's important to stay grounded and realistic when it comes to money matters. Avoid impulsive purchases or investments that seem too good to be true.

The trine between Venus and Saturn on October 4th brings stability and practicality to your financial dealings. This aspect favors long-term financial planning, budgeting, and responsible decision-making. It's a good time to review your financial goals, assess your resources, and make adjustments if necessary. Consider seeking advice from a financial expert or mentor who can provide valuable insights and guidance.

On October 22nd, the square between the Sun and Pluto may bring intense energy to your financial matters. It's crucial to maintain a balanced approach and avoid power struggles or manipulative tactics. Instead, focus on empowerment and taking control of your financial situation. This aspect can also signify a need for transformation and releasing old patterns that no longer serve your financial well-being.

As the month progresses, the sextile between Venus and Pluto on October 24th offers potential for financial growth and opportunities for increasing your wealth. This aspect favors strategic investments, negotiations, and collaborative ventures. Be open to innovative ideas or joint ventures that could lead to financial gains.

Remember to prioritize saving and creating a solid financial foundation for your future. Avoid impulsive spending and focus on long-term financial security. By staying disciplined and making conscious choices, you can navigate the financial landscape with confidence and create a stable and prosperous future.

## Health

The sesquiquadrate aspect between Mercury and Neptune on October 12th may create a need for extra attention to your mental and emotional health. Take time to rest, relax, and engage in activities that promote inner peace and emotional stability. Mindfulness practices, meditation, and journaling can help you navigate any mental fog or confusion that arises.

On October 13th, the square between Mars and Chiron may bring physical or energetic challenges. It's important to listen to your body's signals and avoid pushing yourself too hard. Engage in activities that promote healing, such as gentle exercise, stretching, and self-care routines. Pay attention to your diet and ensure you're nourishing your body with nutritious foods.

The Sun's opposition with Chiron on October 28th highlights the need for self-compassion and self-care. Be mindful of any emotional wounds or vulnerabilities that may arise. Seek support from loved ones, therapists, or support groups if necessary.

Embrace healing modalities that resonate with you, such as therapy, energy work, or holistic practices.

## Travel

The planetary aspects during this month encourage you to step out of your comfort zone, embrace new experiences, and expand your horizons.

The sesquiquadrate aspect between Mercury and Uranus on October 2nd highlights the potential for spontaneous travel or unexpected opportunities to arise. Stay open to new adventures and be flexible with your plans.

On October 8th, the trine between Venus and Mars enhances the spirit of adventure and encourages you to indulge in travel experiences that bring you joy and fulfillment. Whether it's a weekend getaway, a road trip, or a long-distance journey, embrace the thrill of exploring new places and meeting new people.

The biquintile aspect between Mercury and Jupiter on October 23rd enhances your communication skills and intellectual curiosity. It's an excellent time to engage in cultural exchanges, educational trips, or attend workshops and seminars that expand your knowledge and perspectives.

However, be mindful of the quincunx aspect between Mercury and True Node on October 17th, which may introduce some unexpected detours or changes in your travel plans. Maintain a flexible mindset and embrace the journey, even if it deviates from your initial expectations.

As you embark on your travels, remember to prioritize safety and be mindful of any travel restrictions or guidelines. Take necessary precautions and plan ahead to ensure a smooth and enjoyable trip.

Insights from the stars

October is a month of balance, transformation, and depth for Aries. The Libra energy encourages harmony in relationships, while Scorpio calls for introspection and change. Focus on emotional balance, thoughtful decisions, and personal growth.

Best days of the month: October 8th, 12th, 17th, 22nd, 25th, 28th and 31st.

# November 2024

### Horoscope

In November 2024, Aries individuals can expect a dynamic and eventful month filled with opportunities and challenges. The planetary aspects indicate a mix of harmonious alignments and tense influences, urging you to find a balance between your personal desires and responsibilities. This month will require you to embrace your natural leadership skills, assertiveness, and adaptability to make the most of the opportunities that come your way.

The month begins with Jupiter in Gemini forming a sextile with Chiron in Aries on November 2nd. This alignment encourages personal growth and healing through learning and communication. You may find that expanding your knowledge and sharing your experiences can lead to profound healing and newfound wisdom. It's an excellent time to engage in educational pursuits or participate in meaningful conversations that help you understand yourself and others better.

On the same day, Mercury in Scorpio forms a trine with Mars in Cancer, enhancing your communication and mental agility. Your assertiveness and persuasive abilities will be at their peak, allowing you to express your ideas and opinions with clarity and conviction. This aspect favors negotiations, business transactions, and intellectual pursuits. Use this energy to your advantage in professional and personal interactions.

Mercury also forms a sextile with Pluto in Capricorn, bringing depth and intensity to your thought processes. You'll have a keen insight into the underlying motivations and dynamics of situations, making it an excellent time for research, investigative work, or uncovering hidden information. However, be cautious of becoming too obsessed or fixated on certain ideas or beliefs. Balance is key.

Venus also forms a trine with Chiron on the same day, offering opportunities for emotional healing within your relationships. This aspect encourages vulnerability, empathy, and understanding. If there have been past wounds or conflicts, now is the time to address them with compassion and a willingness to find resolutions.

These are just a few of the planetary aspects influencing your November horoscope as an Aries. The month holds a myriad of energies and influences, urging you to be adaptable, mindful, and proactive. By harnessing the strengths of your sign and working with the cosmic energies, you can navigate this month with confidence and achieve your goals.

## Love

In the realm of love, November presents Aries with a blend of exciting possibilities and potential challenges. The opposition between Venus in Sagittarius and Jupiter in Gemini on November 3rd sets the stage for romantic adventures and exploration. You may feel a strong urge to broaden your horizons and seek new experiences within your relationships. This could manifest as a desire for intellectual stimulation or a need for more freedom and independence.

However, it's crucial to maintain open and honest communication with your partner to ensure that your desires align. Discuss your aspirations and aspirations, finding ways to strike a balance between personal growth and the needs of your relationship. Remember that trust and mutual understanding are the foundations of a healthy partnership.

On the same day, Venus forms a trine with Chiron, bringing opportunities for emotional healing and deeper connection. This aspect encourages vulnerability and empathetic understanding within your relationships. It's an ideal time to address any past wounds or unresolved conflicts with your partner, fostering a sense of harmony and closeness.

Throughout the month, be mindful of the potential power struggles and conflicts that may arise due to the Mars-Pluto opposition on November 3rd. These tensions can have an impact on your love life, particularly if you or your partner are asserting control or engaging in manipulative behavior. Practice patience, understanding, and compromise to navigate these challenges successfully.

For single Aries individuals, this month offers opportunities for exciting encounters and new connections. Embrace your adventurous spirit and be open to meeting people from different backgrounds or cultures. However, exercise caution and discernment to ensure that you're aligning with individuals who share your values and long-term goals.

Remember, love requires effort, understanding, and compromise. By embracing the adventurous energy of November and fostering open communication, you can enhance your relationships, deepen your connections, and create a harmonious and fulfilling love life.

## Career

The trine between Mercury in Scorpio and Mars in Cancer on November 2nd empowers your communication skills and mental agility. Your assertiveness and persuasive abilities will be heightened, allowing you to make a compelling case for your ideas and projects. This aspect favors negotiations, presentations, and strategic planning. Use this influential energy to advance your career goals and seek new opportunities.

Furthermore, the sextile between Mercury and Pluto on the same day enhances your analytical and investigative abilities. You'll possess a keen insight into complex matters and be able to uncover hidden information. This can be particularly advantageous if you're involved in research, problem-solving, or any work that requires a deep understanding of underlying dynamics. However, be mindful not to become overly fixated or obsessed with certain ideas or beliefs. Maintain balance and approach your work with an open mind.

The Mars-Pluto opposition on November 3rd introduces a more intense and transformative energy to your professional life. This aspect may bring power struggles, conflicts, or encounters with authority figures. It's essential to avoid becoming overly controlling or manipulative during this period.

Instead, channel your energy into productive pursuits and focus on what you can control. Embrace transformation and be open to letting go of old patterns or beliefs that no longer serve your professional growth.

As November progresses, the opposition between Mercury and Jupiter on November 18th invites expansion and abundance in your career endeavors. This aspect encourages you to think big and have confidence in your abilities. It's a favorable time for networking, seeking mentorship, or exploring new educational opportunities that can enhance your professional skills.

Remember, adaptability, assertiveness, and maintaining a growth mindset are key to capitalizing on the career opportunities that November presents. Embrace the transformative energy and utilize your natural leadership skills to advance your professional aspirations.

## Finance

In the realm of finances, November brings a mixed bag of influences for Aries individuals. While some aspects indicate potential growth and financial opportunities, others suggest the need for caution and careful planning.

The trine between Venus in Sagittarius and Chiron on November 3rd signifies the potential for healing and transformation in your approach to finances. This aspect encourages you to reflect on your past financial patterns and beliefs, allowing you to address any emotional wounds or limiting beliefs that may be holding you back from achieving financial abundance. Consider seeking guidance or education in areas of personal finance to enhance your understanding and make informed decisions.

However, the Venus-Neptune square on November 9th calls for caution in financial matters. It's essential to be realistic and practical when it comes to money. Avoid impulsive spending or making risky investments during this time. Instead, focus on maintaining a balanced budget and prioritizing long-term financial stability.

The Sun's trine with Saturn on November 4th provides a supportive energy for disciplined financial planning and organization. This aspect encourages you to take a responsible approach to your finances, setting clear goals and implementing practical strategies to achieve them. Consider seeking advice from financial professionals or mentors who can provide valuable insights and guidance.

Throughout the month, it's crucial to maintain a mindful and balanced approach to your financial decisions. Consider saving and investing for the long term, while also allowing yourself some well-deserved rewards for your hard work. Stay informed about market trends and make informed choices that align with your financial goals.

## Health

The opposition between Mars in Cancer and Pluto on November 3rd may bring heightened intensity and potential power struggles, which can impact your overall stress levels. It's crucial to find healthy outlets to channel this energy, such as engaging in regular exercise, practicing mindfulness techniques, or seeking professional support if needed. Taking proactive measures to manage stress will contribute to your overall health and well-being.

The Sun's trine with Neptune on November 4th provides an opportunity for spiritual and emotional healing. This aspect encourages you to engage in activities that nourish your soul and promote inner peace. Consider incorporating practices such as meditation, yoga, or spending time in nature to enhance your overall well-being.

Maintaining a balanced and nutritious diet is essential during this time. Pay attention to your body's needs and ensure you're providing it with the necessary nutrients. Consider incorporating stress-relieving foods, such as omega-3 fatty acids, leafy greens, and foods rich in antioxidants, into your diet.

It's also important to prioritize rest and rejuvenation. Create a soothing bedtime routine and aim for quality sleep each night. Adequate rest will contribute to your overall vitality and energy levels.

Remember to listen to your body's signals and address any concerns promptly. If you're experiencing persistent health issues, consider seeking professional medical advice to ensure proper care and treatment.

## Travel

Whether it's for leisure or professional purposes, traveling during this month can be rewarding and enlightening.

The sextile between Jupiter in Gemini and Chiron on November 2nd suggests that travel can play a role in your personal growth and healing journey. Exploring new places, cultures, and ideas can broaden your perspective and offer valuable insights. Consider planning a trip that aligns with your interests and provides opportunities for learning and self-discovery.

The Sun's sextile with Pluto on November 21st enhances the transformative potential of your travels. You may find yourself drawn to destinations that offer profound experiences or have a significant historical or spiritual significance. Embrace the opportunities for personal growth and self-reflection that travel can provide during this time.

When traveling, be mindful of your physical and mental well-being. Maintain a balanced approach to your activities, allowing for both exploration and relaxation. Take breaks when needed and engage in activities that promote rejuvenation and self-care.

Additionally, pay attention to practical considerations such as travel arrangements, safety precautions, and adhering to local customs and regulations. Proper planning and organization will ensure a smooth and enjoyable travel experience.

Whether you're embarking on a short getaway or a more extended journey, keep an open mind and embrace the adventures that come your way. Travel can be a transformative experience, offering new perspectives, personal growth, and cherished memories.

Insights from the stars

This November, the stars are aligning to offer Aries an opportunity for deep transformation and adventurous expansion. This is a time to break out of your comfort zone and embrace the unknown.

Best days of the month: November 2nd, 4th, 9th, 18th, 19th, 23rd, 27th.

## December 2024

### Horoscope

This month urges you to tap into your inner strength, embrace change, and navigate challenges with confidence and resilience. The planetary aspects highlight the need for balance, adaptability, and self-reflection as you move forward on your journey.

The month begins with Venus forming a biquintile with Jupiter on December 1st, setting a harmonious tone for love and abundance. This aspect encourages you to cultivate gratitude and optimism, attracting positive experiences and deepening your connections with loved ones.

Mercury's trine with Chiron on December 2nd enhances your communication skills and brings opportunities for emotional healing. This aspect supports open and honest conversations, making it an ideal time to address any past wounds or conflicts within your relationships.

The opposition between Venus and Mars on December 12th brings a mix of passion and tension to your love life. It's important to find a balance between assertiveness and compromise in your relationships.

Avoid power struggles and aim for open and respectful communication.

The Sun's square with Neptune on December 18th may bring a sense of confusion or uncertainty. It's important to stay grounded and maintain realistic expectations. Be cautious when making financial decisions or entering into new agreements. Take time for self-reflection and seek clarity before committing to major choices.

As December comes to a close, Mercury's trine with Chiron on December 31st provides opportunities for emotional healing and personal growth. Reflect on the lessons learned throughout the year and release any emotional baggage that may be holding you back. This aspect offers a fresh start and renewed optimism as you enter the new year.

In summary, December 2024 calls for Aries individuals to embrace their inner strength and navigate challenges with grace. Focus on open communication, adaptability, and maintaining a balanced approach to relationships and responsibilities. Stay grounded and practice self-care as you move through this transformative month.

## Love

The biquintile aspect between Venus and Jupiter on December 1st infuses your love life with joy, optimism, and a sense of abundance. This alignment encourages you to appreciate the blessings in your relationships and nurture a spirit of gratitude. Embrace the positive energy and create memorable moments with your partner.

However, the square between Venus and Uranus on December 28th introduces some unpredictability and potential disruptions in your love life. It's important to be open-minded and flexible, as unexpected changes may require you to adapt and find new ways to connect with your partner. Embrace the opportunities for growth and deepen your understanding of each other's needs and desires.

The Sun's semi-square with Venus on December 11th may create minor tensions and challenges in your relationships. It's crucial to find a balance between your personal aspirations and the needs of your partner. Seek compromise and open communication to maintain harmony and avoid misunderstandings.

For single Aries individuals, this month invites exploration and self-reflection in matters of the heart. Embrace the transformative energy of December to release any emotional baggage and old patterns that may have hindered your ability to attract and nurture meaningful connections. Trust in the process of personal growth and have faith that the right person will come into your life at the right time.

## Career

The planetary aspects indicate the need for adaptability, perseverance, and a strategic approach to achieve your career goals.

Mercury's opposition with Jupiter on December 4th may bring potential challenges and conflicting viewpoints in your work environment. It's important to remain open-minded and receptive to different perspectives. Engage in constructive conversations and seek solutions that benefit all parties involved.

The Sun's square with Saturn on the same day emphasizes the need for discipline and responsibility in your career endeavors. This aspect may bring increased demands and obligations, testing your patience and commitment. Embrace these challenges as opportunities for growth and strive for excellence in your work.

The semi-square between the Sun and Venus on December 11th may introduce minor tensions or distractions in your professional life. It's essential to maintain focus and avoid getting caught up in office politics or unnecessary conflicts. Stay dedicated to your goals and align your actions with your long-term aspirations.

The biquintile aspect between the Sun and Mars on December 20th ignites your drive and ambition. Use this energy to take proactive steps towards achieving your career objectives. Embrace new challenges, seek opportunities for advancement, and showcase your leadership skills.

Throughout December, it's important to maintain a balanced approach to your career. Stay organized, prioritize tasks, and seek support when needed. Embrace the transformative energy of the month to reassess your professional path and make necessary adjustments.

### Finance

The square between Venus and Uranus on December 28th may introduce some unpredictability and potential financial disruptions. It's important to have contingency plans and be prepared for unexpected expenses or changes in your financial situation. Avoid impulsive spending and focus on building a solid financial foundation.

The semi-square between Venus and Saturn on December 5th emphasizes the need for financial responsibility and discipline. Be mindful of your budget and prioritize long-term financial stability over short-term gratification. Consider seeking professional advice or guidance in managing your finances effectively.

The semi-square between Venus and Neptune on December 17th calls for caution in financial matters. Be wary of any offers or investments that seem too good to be true. Exercise discernment and seek clarity before making any major financial decisions. Protect your assets and avoid unnecessary risks.

Throughout December, it's important to focus on practicality and long-term financial goals. Set clear financial objectives and create a budget that allows for both saving and responsible spending. Practice self-discipline and avoid unnecessary expenses that may hinder your financial progress.

## Health

The semi-square between the Sun and Mars on December 12th may bring heightened energy levels and a sense of restlessness. It's important to channel this energy productively through regular exercise and physical activities. Engage in activities that promote strength, endurance, and stress relief.

The Sun's quincunx with Uranus on December 15th may create a sense of restlessness or unease. It's crucial to pay attention to your mental and emotional well-being during this time. Practice mindfulness techniques, such as meditation or deep breathing exercises, to find inner calm and balance.

The square between the Sun and Neptune on December 18th emphasizes the importance of maintaining a healthy lifestyle. Be mindful of your dietary choices and ensure that you're nourishing your body with nutritious foods. Aim for a balanced diet that includes plenty of fruits, vegetables, lean proteins, and whole grains.

Throughout December, prioritize rest and rejuvenation. Establish a soothing bedtime routine and aim for quality sleep each night. Proper rest is essential for replenishing your energy levels and supporting overall well-being.

If you're experiencing any persistent health concerns, it's advisable to seek professional medical advice. Be proactive in addressing any issues and follow recommended treatments or therapies.

## Travel

The biquintile between Venus and Jupiter on December 1st creates a harmonious and joyful energy for travel. This aspect encourages you to embrace new experiences, broaden your horizons, and connect with different cultures and perspectives. Consider planning a trip that aligns with your interests and offers opportunities for personal growth.

The Sun's biquintile with Uranus on December 21st infuses your travels with excitement and unexpected adventures. Embrace the spontaneity and allow yourself to step out of your comfort zone. This is a favorable time for exploring new destinations or engaging in unique experiences that broaden your perspective.

When traveling in December, it's important to prioritize self-care and well-being. Take breaks when needed and engage in activities that promote relaxation and rejuvenation. Be mindful of your personal safety and adhere to any travel advisories or regulations in the places you visit.

Consider incorporating mindful practices into your travel routine, such as meditation, journaling, or connecting with nature. These practices can enhance your travel experiences, promote self-reflection, and allow you to fully immerse yourself in the transformative energy of your journeys.

Whether you're embarking on a short getaway or a more extended adventure, keep an open mind and embrace the opportunities for personal growth and self-discovery that travel brings. Allow yourself to be

# 116 · COMPLETE ARIES 2024 PERSONAL HOROSCOPE

present in each moment, connect with the people you meet, and create lasting memories.

Insights from the stars

The stars in December bring a blend of adventurous and disciplined energies for Aries. Utilize the Sagittarian energy for exploration and the Capricorn energy for setting solid foundations for the future. Reflect on the past year and set your intentions for the year ahead.

Best days of the month: December 2nd, 10th, 13th, 19th, 23rd, 24th and 31st.

Printed by Amazon Italia Logistica S.r.l.
Torrazza Piemonte (TO), Italy